Contemporary Praise for Ladies' Voices

Arranged for Trio, Ensemble, or Choir

By Dennis Allen

lillenas
PUBLISHING COMPANY
lillenas.com

Contents

Speechless

Words and Music by
STEVEN CURTIS CHAPMAN
and **GEOFF MOORE**
Arranged by Russell Mauldin
S.S.A. arrangement by Dennis Allen

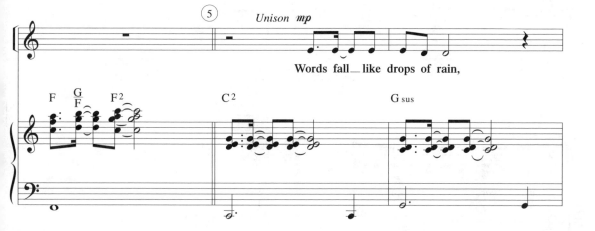

PLEASE NOTE: Copying of this product is NOT covered by CCLI licenses. For CCLI information call 1-800-234-2446.

man - y things, try - ing____ to fig - ure____ You out.

But, as mer - cy o - pens____ my eyes,

my words____ are stol - en____ a - way With this

breath - tak - ing view of____ Your grace. And I am

CD: 4

God of this whole u - ni - verse. It's a

story that's too great for words. And I am

speech - less, I'm as - ton - ished and a - mazed. I am

si - lenced by Your won-drous grace; You have saved me, You have

11

On My Cross

Words and Music by
JEREMY DEIBLER
Arranged by Dennis Allen

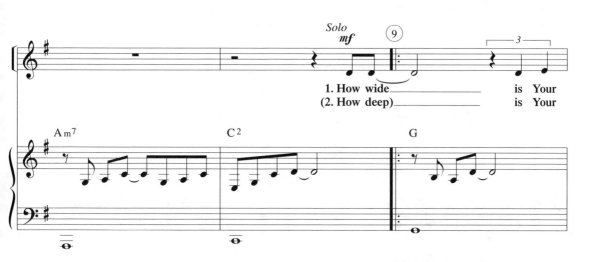

1. How wide_____ is Your
(2. How deep)_____ is Your

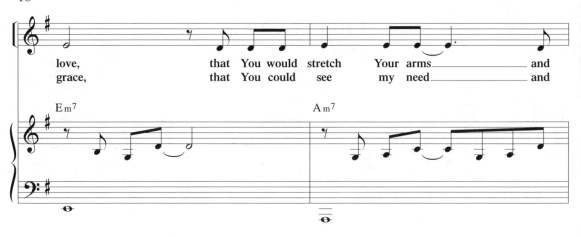

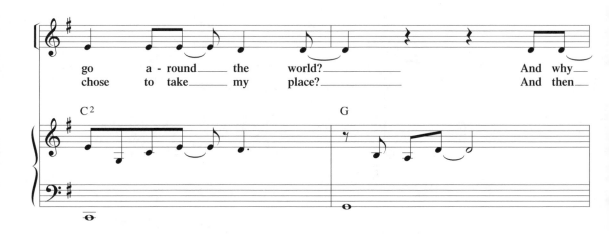

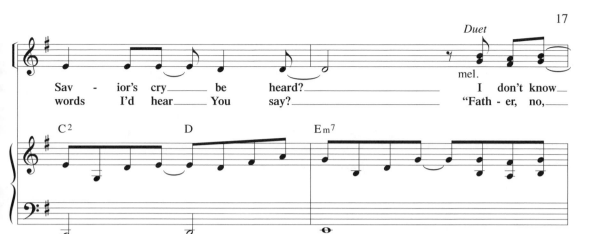

Sav - ior's cry_____ be heard?_____ I don't know_
words I'd hear_____ You say?_____ "Fath - er, no,_

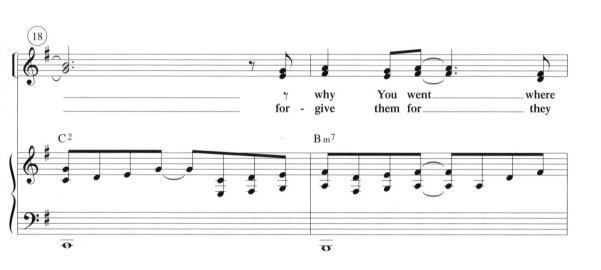

_____ why You went_____where
for - give them for_____they

I was meant_____ to go._____ I don't know_
know not what_____ they do._____ I will go_

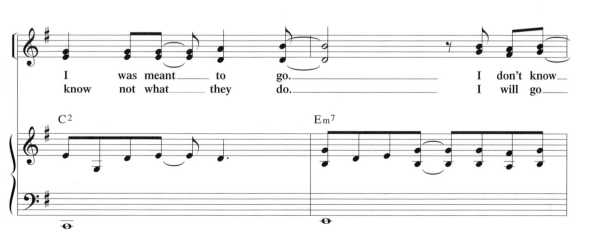

Leaning on the Everlasting Arms

ELISHA HOFFMAN

ANTHONY SHOWALTER
Arranged by Dennis Allen

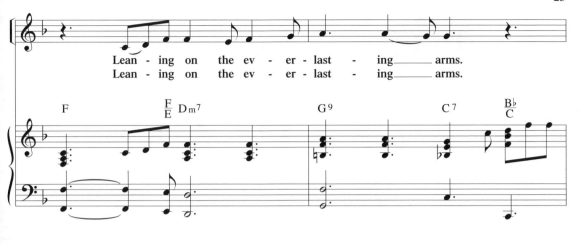

Lean - ing on the ev - er - last - ing____ arms.
Lean - ing on the ev - er - last - ing____ arms.

What a bless - ed - ness, what a peace is mine,
O how bright the path grows from day to day,

CD: 13 1st time
CD: 15 2nd time

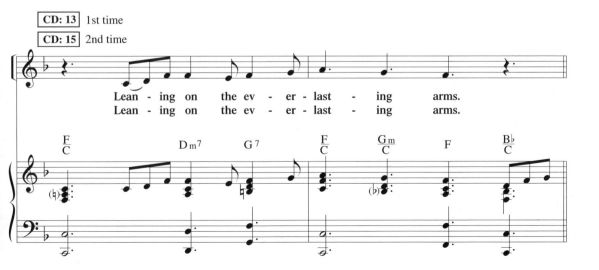

Lean - ing on the ev - er - last - ing arms.
Lean - ing on the ev - er - last - ing arms.

lean - ing, lean-ing on the ev - er - last - ing arms?

mp

Oo

I___ have a bless-ed peace___with my Lord, my Lord so near,___'Cause I'm

CD: 17

lean - ing___ on the ev - er - last - ing___ arms.

Oo

New Mercies

Words and Music by
DENNIS and NAN ALLEN
Arranged by Dennis Allen

- ing, day af-ter day.

New mer-

New mer - cies ev - 'ry day.

- cies ev - 'ry day.

New mer - cies ev - 'ry day.

New mer - cies.

Sing Praise to God Who Reigns Above

JOHANN J. SCHUTZ
tr. by FRANCES E. COX

Kirchengesänge, 1566
and DENNIS ALLEN
Arranged by Dennis Allen

praise to___ God!___ Be joy-ful in the Lord, my heart! Both

soul and bod-y bear your part: To God all___ praise___ and

glo - ry!_____ glo - ry! Sing___ Praise!___ The Lord___ is nev - er

far a - way._____ far a - way. An ev - er - pres - ent,

ev - er - pre - sent help and stay, An ev - er - pres - ent

help and stay._____ Let all who___ name, who name Christ's

ho - ly___ name Give___ God all___ praise___ and glo -

ry; Sing praise, sing praise to God! Let all who own, who own His

pow'r pro - claim A - loud the won - drous

sto - ry. Sing praise, sing praise to God! Cast

ev - 'ry i - dol from its throne, For Christ is Lord, and Christ a -

lone: To God all praise and glo -

ry! Sing praise! To God all praise and glo -

ry! Sing praise! Praise, sing praise! Praise!

Desire of My Heart

BEVERLY DARNALL

JEFF SLAUGHTER
Arranged by Camp Kirkland
S.S.A. arrangement by Dennis Allen

1. How could I know_____ You____
2. How could He know_____ I____

__ would love me so, And see in me a child to call__

__ could walk this road That bro't me to this mo - ment here__

Eb2   Gb2

__ Your own?__ ⁊ All I'll ev - er need is

__ and now?__ What - ev - er you must do, His

GbM7   Eb2

wait - ing here for me, ⁊ Hid - den in the heart of You__

prom - is - es are true His love will hold me up some - way,__

Eb2   Gb2

Je - sus, You are all _____ the de - si-

- re of _____ my ____ heart. _____

And I won-dered what the pur - pose of my life was un -

48

Heart of Worship Medley

The Heart of Worship
My Jesus, I Love Thee
Fairest Lord Jesus
O Come, Let Us Adore Him

Arranged by Dennis Allen

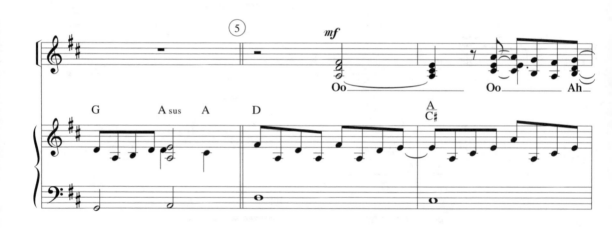

*"The Heart of Worship"
Choir and congregation

CD: 28

52

54

I'm com-ing back to the heart,___ the heart___ of wor-

ship.___

*"Fairest Lord Jesus"
Choir and congregation

Fair - est Lord Je - sus! Rul - er of all na - ture!

O___ Thou of God and___ man the

Son! _____ Thee will I cher - ish;

Thee will I hon - or, Thou, my soul's glo - ry,

joy, and crown! O

*"O Come, Let Us Adore Him"

come, let us a - dore Him, _____ O

Choir only

come, let us a - dore Him. O for He a-lone is wor - thy, And we'll give Him all the glo - ry, the glo - ry!

Forever

Words and Music by
CHRIS TOMLIN
Arranged by Michael Lawrence
S.S.A. arrangement by Dennis Allen

God and King; His love en - dures for - ev -

G

- er. For He is good He is a -

G   C²

bove all things; His love en - dures for - ev -

C²

- er. Sing praise, sing

G   D

The Father's Song

Words and Music by
MATT REDMAN
Arranged by Dennis Allen

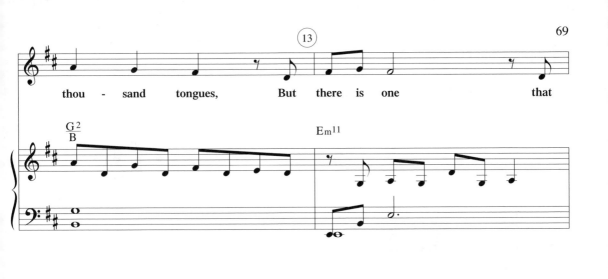

thou - sand tongues, But there is one that

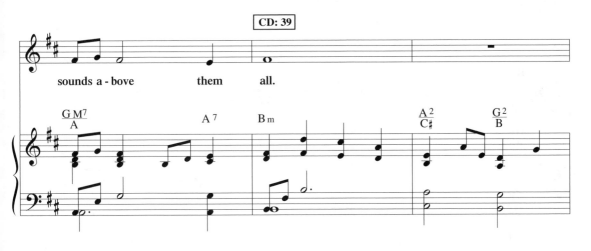

CD: 39

sounds a - bove them all.

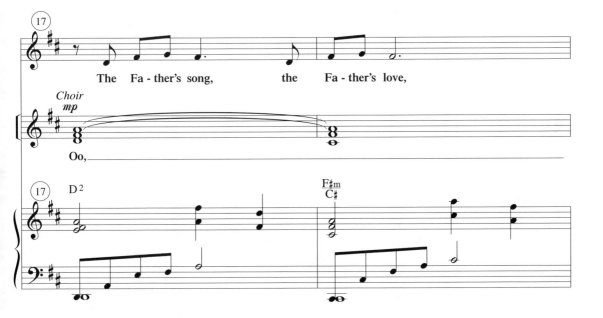

The Fa - ther's song, the Fa - ther's love,

Choir
mp

Oo,

69

70

O for a Thousand Tongues to Sing

CHARLES WESLEY

CARL G. GLASER
and DENNIS ALLEN
Arranged by Dennis Allen

CD: 47

sets the pris - 'ner free. His blood can make the

C m7   B♭m11   E♭7   A♭M7

CD: 48

foul - est clean; His blood a - vailed for____

G♭°7   Fm11

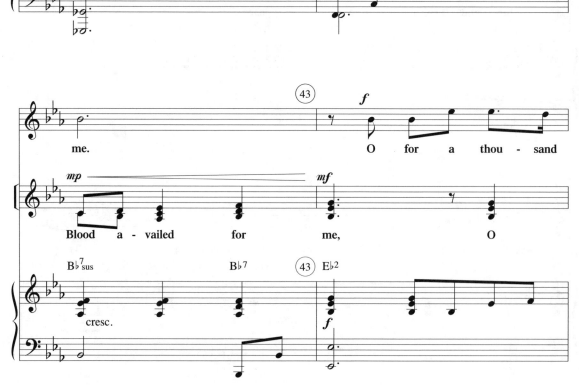

me.   O for a thou - sand

f

mp _____ **mf**

Blood a - vailed for me,   O

B♭7sus   B♭7   (43) E♭2

cresc.   **f**

Hallelujah (Your Love Is Amazing)

Words and Music by
BRENTON BROWN
and **BRIAN DOERKSEN**
Arranged by Dennis Allen

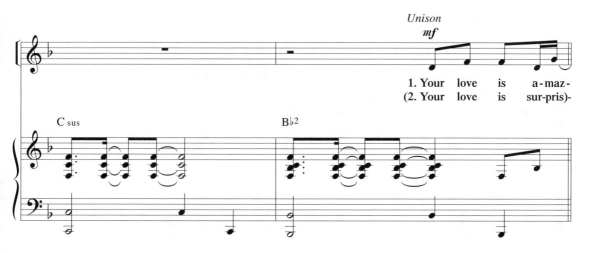

1. Your love is a-maz-
(2. Your love is sur-pris)-

-ing, stead-y and un-chang - ing. Your love is a moun-
-ing, I can feel it ris - ing. All the joy that's grow-

- tain, firm be-neath___ my feet. Your love is a mys-
- ing deep in-side___ of me. Ev - 'ry time I see___

CD: 51 1st time

CD: 53 2nd time

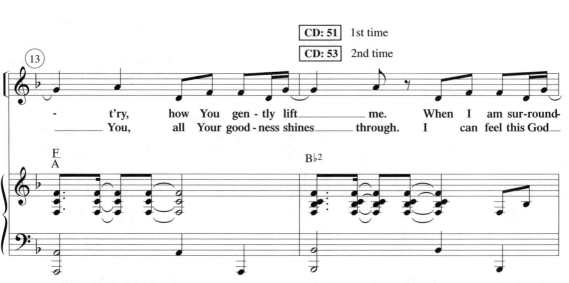

- t'ry, how You gen - tly lift_____ me. When I am sur-round-
_____ You, all Your good - ness shines_____ through. I can feel this God

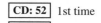

Bow the Knee

Words and Music by
CHRIS MACHEN and
MIKE HARLAND
Arranged by Tom Fettke
S.S.A. arrangement by Dennis Allen

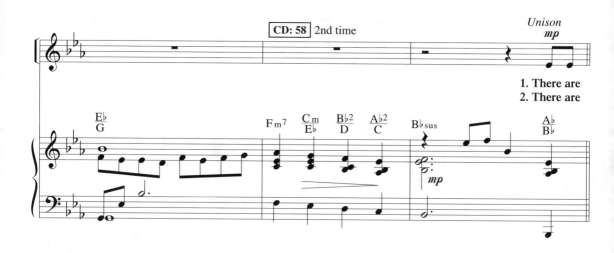

The lyrics in measure 7:

1. mo - ments on our jour - ney_____ fol - low - ing____ the Lord– Where
2. days when clouds sur - round us,_____ and the rain be - gins____ to fall, The

God il - lu - mines ev - 'ry step we take. There are
cold and lone - ly winds won't cease to blow. And there

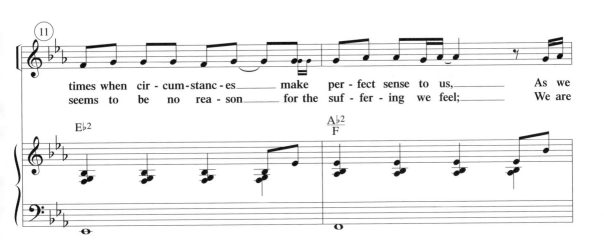

times when cir - cum - stanc - es make per - fect sense to us, As we
seems to be no rea - son for the suf - fer - ing we feel; We are

try to un - der - stand each move He makes. When the
tempt - ed to be - lieve God does not know. When the

path_____ grows dim And our
storms_____ a - rise, Don't for -

CD: 57 1st time
CD: 59 2nd time

ques-tions have no an-swers, turn to Him._____
get we live by faith and not by sight._____

rit.

20 A little faster ♩ = ca. 69

Bow the knee; trust the heart of your Fa-ther when the

rit.

Faster

98

You Are My King

Words and Music by
BILLY JAMES FOOTE
Arranged by Dennis Allen

With emotion ♩ = ca. 70

I'm for-giv-en be-cause You were for-sak-en.

I'm ac-cept-ed, You were con-demned.

There Is Joy Medley

There Is Joy in the Lord
Joyful, Joyful, We Adore Thee
Rejoice, the Lord Is King
Joy to the World

Arranged by Dennis Allen

10 𝄋 *"There Is Joy in the Lord"

112

The Lord Is the Strength of My Life

Words and Music by
CHRIS MACHEN
Arranged by Dennis Allen

life, of whom shall I be a-

fraid.

The

fraid?

Tho' the

We Fall Down

Words and Music by
CHRIS TOMLIN
Arranged by Dennis Allen

Wait

Words and Music by
DENNIS and NAN ALLEN
Arranged by Dennis Allen

Wait, wait, wait, wait on the Lord. Wait for Him pa-tient-ly and He'll lift you up. He'll lift you

The Call

Words and Music by
KIRK KIRKLAND,
DENNIS and NAN ALLEN
Arranged by Dennis Allen

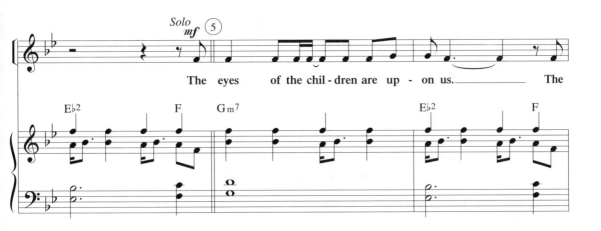

The eyes of the chil - dren are up - on us._____ The

ears of the world___ are tuned our way,

look - ing and lis - t'ning for ev - i - dence,_____ ex -

am - in-ing____ the fab - ric of____ our faith.

Choir unison

Do they

see us hold - ing firm____ in our con - vic - tions?_____ Do they

Divisi

see us mov - ing for - ward in the cause? Do they

CD: 90

rise and an-swer the call.

We're wo-ven to-geth-er as a tap-es-try,_____ e-ven tho' each strand is dif-f'rent from the rest._____ We be-

come a thing of beau - ty and of strength. When we're

held to-geth - er by a com-mon thread. *Choir unison* So let us

put a-side___ those things that would di - vide___ us,___ let us

Divisi press on to the goal___ to which we're called. The great - est

146

All Creatures of Our God and King

FRANCIS OF ASSISI
tr. by WILLIAM H. DRAPER

Geistliche Kirchengesange
and DENNIS ALLEN
Arranged by Dennis Allen

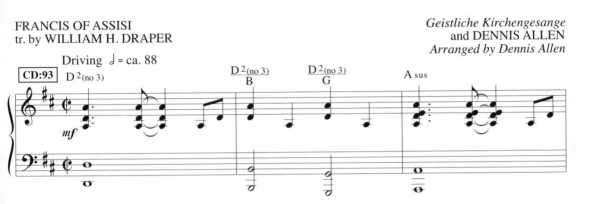

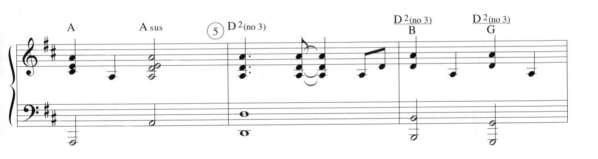

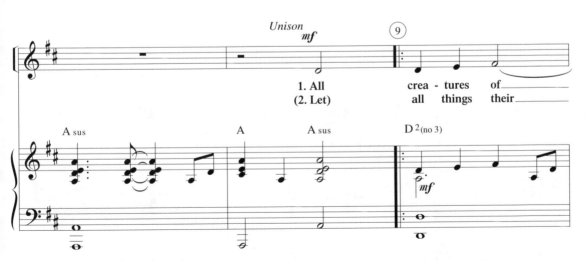

our God and King, Lift
Cre - a - tor bless, And

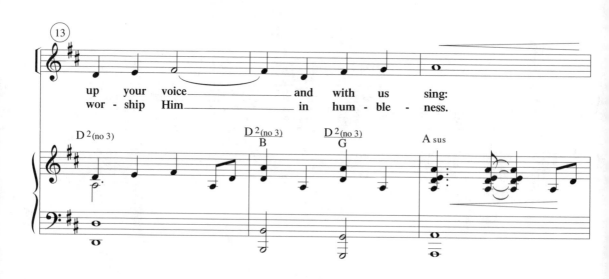

up your voice_____ and with us sing:
wor - ship Him_____ in hum - ble - ness.

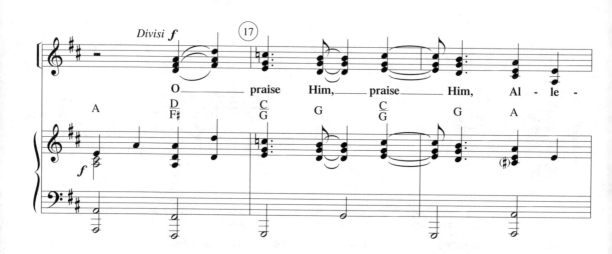

O_____ praise Him,_____ praise_____ Him, Al - le -

CD: 94 1st time
CD: 96 2nd time

lu - ia! ___ O ___ praise Him, ___ praise ___ Him, Al - le - lu - ia! ___ Thou Praise, burn - ing sun ___ with gold - en beam, praise the Fa - ther, praise the Son,

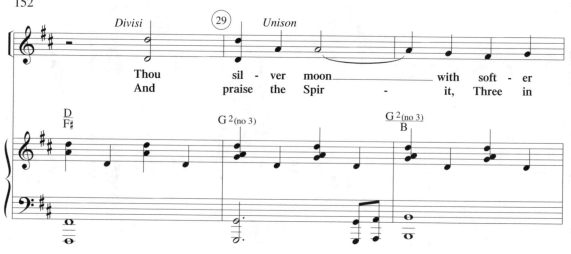

(to pg. 149, meas. 9)

160